# TRANSFORMING DEPRESSION INTO A PROSPEROUS LIFE

## UNVEILING YOUR INNER TRUTH

### Michael Chavez

Daniel Gomez L.L.C

Transforming Depression into a Prosperous Life: Unveiling Your Inner Truth

by Michael Chavez

Published by Daniel Gomez Enterprises LLC / December 2025

Contact Info: (210) 663-5954 / Email: Info@DanielGomezGlobal.com

Copyright © 2025, Michael Chavez

All rights reserved.

ISBN 978-1-970549-01-0

All rights reserved. No part of this book may be used or reproduced by any means, graphic, electronic, or mechanical, including photocopying, recording, taping, or by any other means of information storage retrieval system, without the express written permission of the author, except in the case of brief quotations.
The content is the sole expression and opinion of its author. No warranties or guarantees are expressed or implied by the content herein. Neither the publisher nor the author shall be liable for any physical, psychological, emotional, financial, or commercial damages, including, but not limited to, special, incidental, consequential, or other damages.

# Dedication

This book is dedicated to God.

# Table of Contents

| | |
|---|---|
| Introduction | 11 |
| Chapter 1: The Hidden Power | 13 |
| Chapter 2: Life in the Valley | 24 |
| Chapter 3: Tapping into Power Within | 34 |
| Chapter 4: Forgiveness | 42 |
| Chapter 5: A Grateful Heart | 52 |
| Chapter 6: Write Your Own Story | 60 |
| Chapter 7: Unconditional Love | 66 |
| Chapter 8: Your Circle Matters | 76 |
| Chapter 9: The Source | 82 |
| Conclusion | 88 |

# Introduction

Life is a season of ups and downs—hills and valleys, mountaintop victories. My hope is that as you read *Transforming Depression into a Prosperous Life*, you are reading it from a high place, from the mountaintop. But if you find yourself in a valley right now, my hope is that this book will encourage you, inspire you, and help you realize that you are more powerful than you think you are, and that you bring more value than you ever imagined.

When I transitioned from military life to civilian life, I found myself in some deep valleys. I was depressed. I doubted myself. I couldn't find my way out. But the more I searched, the more I realized there was a true identity hidden inside of me—waiting to be discovered.

Get out your pen and paper, because I know this book is going to bless you. Read it as if you're going to teach it to someone else. I believe it's going to make a difference in who you are.

## Chapter 1

# The Hidden Power

"With God all things are possible." Matthew 19:26

There is a hidden power deep inside of you that no one else can identify or take away. It cannot be destroyed or altered. But this is something you must discover for yourself. This brings to mind the elephant—an animal capable of uprooting trees but conditioned, from a young age, to believe it is held by a simple rope. Born in captivity, elephants are tethered while they're still small, too weak to break free. Over time, they stop trying, conditioned to think the rope is stronger than their own strength. The truth is, it's not the rope that holds them—it's their belief.

This hidden power, which you possess, is greater than the physical strength of the elephant. What is this power? It is your mind. Your mind can either solve problems or create problems. This is dependent on where you place your focus. No one was promised to have an easy life without trials and tribulations. It is the ability and the desire of the individual to see the opportunity in adversity. Where does this power come from?

The words you speak are more powerful than you realize. Your words can strengthen or weaken someone else's spirit as well as your own. It has been proven that a child raised receiving praise, encouragement, and guidance grows up with a higher self-esteem than a child raised with criticism. There are people I know who strive to earn the approval of a parent even in their adult years because of a lack of self-esteem. It is the desire to be validated by other people which keep many from achieving their full potential.

When I was younger, I grew tired of the criticism received from my family and people around me. This caused me to not only build walls but pushed me to prove people wrong when they said I would fail. It gave a sense of pride and accomplishment. Still, it took a toll on my esteem. Constantly being told you are not good enough eventually programs your beliefs about your value and worth. Eventually, I became cynical, and rigid to the point where I refused guidance when it was given. Learning to be coachable is a new challenge to overcome for personal growth. Today, I'm learning to receive feedback without defensiveness, recognizing that guidance isn't criticism—it's a gift from those who want to see me succeed.

We are all ignorant of a great many things. We are conditioned to judge ignorance as a fault. It is both a fault and a gift depending on your perspective. Embrace ignorance as an opportunity to grow, to learn, and to understand the problems you face. You have a natural curiosity but have been conditioned to set it on a shelf and focus on the business of the day. To remain ignorant is a fault which hinders opportunities for growth, learning, and success.

We are each gifted with unique, specific talents and abilities no one else possesses. Examine the people you are surrounded by and notice there are some who are well organized, some are excellent communicators, some have a natural eye for talent in other people. It is written in the Bible, King Solomon asked God for wisdom. God joyfully blessed Solomon and made him the wisest man who ever existed. Understanding your gifts will propel you to achieving your heart's desires.

"What is the difference between people who succeed and those who fail?" This is one of many questions I asked when I started the journey of personal development. There is a young woman by the name of Taya Smith who became the face of Hillsong United, an Australian Christian worship group. There is one song in particular which she sings that moved me and drew me into listening to their music. One day an acoustic version of this song was played on YouTube.

As I watched and listened, I could see Taya was pouring herself into this song. It brought me to appreciate it more than before. The song title is "Oceans" which is about going into the deep water, the unknown and stepping out in faith. There was a short clip of Taya's story which is only the beginning to the answer to my question. She came from a farm in Australia with $200 in her pocket and bet on herself.

The evidence of her commitment to pouring herself into the music has propelled her to the international stage. The humility in her voice as she ended the short interview said all I needed to know. Success comes from selfless giving to others for a noble purpose. Successful people dedicate their lives to perfecting their skills, their talents for their craft. They do this as a commitment to offering the best version of themselves.

Before I got into personal development I had become committed to playing an online video game. This occupied my time throughout the day and evening to the point I neglected personal matters. One particular evening a thought came to me, "What kind of business could I build if I spent as much time and energy on it as I do this game?" Recognizing how those who earn more are committed to their profession and developing the discipline required for success. In short, examining my own lack of success and income. This question brought me to pursue my dream of having my own business. This is how I came into coaching. Being able to influence others to succeed is something I am passionate about as it is what I see as my purpose in life. It is my desire to succeed, not just in my own business, but in helping others. It is about leadership by example. To be an effective leader, becoming an intelligent follower attracts others to trust you.

Most people rely solely on their five senses—sight, touch, taste, hearing, smell—to navigate life. But your perspective is limited by the beliefs you've inherited. While you can't change your genetics, you can change your environment and, more importantly, your thinking.

There are a number of stories of successful people coming from a life of poverty to a life of abundance. It is not impossible except in the mind of the individual.

There are six higher faculties which have been gifted to us as well. They are memory, perception, imagination, reason, intuition, and the will. These faculties are tools to help you unlock your hidden power. By consciously developing them, you'll not only improve your mind, but also gain greater control over your life and its direction. It takes committed effort, study, and a desire for something more. You were not created to merely exist but to experience the abundance in life. What is the one thing you dream of? The thing which speaks to you in your imagination?

Your imagination is both your best gift and your worst enemy. It is directed by your belief system. It is just as easy to imagine success as it is to imagine failure. Think of your dreams as you sleep. Some of them are uplifting and inspiring while others leave you scared or curious. Often times the imagination is used against you. Especially when you watch the news, listen to the radio, or talk to someone who paints a negative picture of impending troubles.

Your mind does not know the difference between real or imagined. This has been discovered and proven through various studies into the mind and the brain. This is why being selective in the information you entertain is of great importance. Spiritual, mental, and physical health are key for this hidden power within. It is about self-control and the decisions you make in various aspects of your life.

But here's what most people won't admit: it's not failure they're actually imagining—it's fear. Fear of judgment. Fear of losing what little security they have. Fear of discovering they're not who they thought they were. What fear has you by the rope right now? For me, it was the fear of rejection. There were many times where I had to have a few drinks before I would ask a woman to dance. It was the fear of rejection and being laughed at because I felt awkward dancing in a crowd. I still feel uncomfortable dancing but can now approach women with confidence. Learning who I am through reading the Bible, personal development, and accepting myself despite my flaws is what built my confidence. This sounds harsh, but it is okay if people choose not to like you. I realized the worst that could happen was a 'no'—and I'd survived plenty of those. The fear was always bigger than the reality. Be honest. Is it fear of failure, or is it actually fear of success and the responsibility that comes with it? Name your fear. Look directly at it. Because an unnamed fear controls you, while a named fear can be faced.

Morris Goodman "The Miracle Man" was a successful businessman who crashed his plane in March 1981. He was paralyzed from the neck down, unable to speak, eat, swallow, or breath on his own. The doctors said he would end up as a vegetable who could only blink his eyes. To their surprise, he was consciously aware of the conversations. He tells of how he was determined to walk out of the hospital by Christmas that year on his own.

I first heard of his story as I was watching the movie, "The Secret" which was based on the book written by Rhonda Byrne. His is not the only story of the healing power of the mind and body from fatal accidents. Dr. Joe Dispenza is another amazing story of the healing power of the mind and body.

Dr. Joe Dispenza tells of experience of healing six vertebrae which were shattered while competing in a triathlon in Southern California. He was 23 years old at the time. The orthopedic specialists who viewed the X-rays and MRI reports each recommended a surgery using a Harrington rod to repair the damage to his back otherwise he would be paralyzed for life. Each doctor who he saw offered the same prognosis and recommended the surgery.

Dr. Dispenza opted not to have the surgery. Instead, he went through the process of healing his body mentally. For many the healing power of the body is a mystery. When you cut yourself or break a bone, the body already knows how to heal itself. When you read the labels on the medications you purchase over the counter or receive through a prescription each say the same thing. That it only treats the symptoms of the illness and not the cause.

"You have power over your mind, not outside events." Marcus Aurelius, Roman Emperor. How you control the direction of your life is based on how you control your mind and the thoughts you entertain. This hidden power can be used to your advantage when you understand it exists. I never knew existed until I started asking questions. Why do people do the things they do? Why, is the best question to ask followed by "Is this true?" Remember, your imagination can work against you. You have the power to either accept or reject the information you receive. The poet who wrote Invictus ended with the following line, "I am the master of my fate. I am the captain of my soul." It was a powerful ending, even more so when you take time to understand the meaning. It goes back to you having the power to control your mind and your higher faculties.

"It's not what happens to you but how you react to it that matters." Epictetus, Greek Stoic Philosopher. Rush hour traffic is something which used to stress me out. Not understanding as to why people feel the need to tailgate or cut off other drivers because they are not paying attention to their exit. Anger is an easy emotion to express as it is more of a habit than anything. It was easy for me to complain about my experiences on the road.

It is when I was introduced to personal development and many of the books on the mind, imagination, metaphysics, and self-image psychology which helped me overcome the limitations which held me hostage. You have the power to control the direction of your life both on a personal and professional level. The most successful people experience problems in their lives like everyone else.

You've already proven this power exists within you, even if you haven't recognized it yet. Think back to a specific moment when you achieved something meaningful despite the odds. I never learned how to swim when I was growing up. Which is comical since I enlisted in the Navy after graduation. Knowing how to swim was not a requirement. They taught us how to float in basic training as it is key to survival if you fall overboard from a ship. When I was stationed aboard small craft we were required to be a qualified second-class swimmer. This was where I failed. The command sent me to school to obtain the qualification. This was necessary, but it meant an entire week of training in the pool. One thing I learned from this experience is that despite my best efforts I cannot sink. This was really helpful because being relaxed in the water is necessary to swim. Learning to let go of your fears is one of many keys for success. Remember that moment. How did it feel when the skeptics were proven wrong? That wasn't luck. That was your hidden power breaking through the conditioning, the doubt, the limitations others tried to place on you. You've accessed this power before. The question is: will you access it again, intentionally this time?

"We cannot choose our external circumstances, but we can always choose how we respond to them." Epictetus, Greek Stoic Philosopher. Your power comes from within, when you learn this concept of self-mastery the world of opportunities will come easier. This is not to say adversity is nullified, growth comes at a price. The wisdom you gain from overcoming adversity increases mental strength.

The dreams which have been placed before you are not there by accident. Pursuing a worthwhile goal is about becoming a better version of yourself. This new version is what you are really seeking. How many times have you heard someone say, "I am trying to find myself."? The answer comes from within and not the without.

You already possess everything you need. The power is there, waiting. It has always been there. I learned to swim at 28 years old in the Navy not because I suddenly became coordinated, but because I stopped believing I would sink. The same power that taught you to walk without instruction, that heals your body without conscious effort, is the power that will carry you toward your dreams.

The only question remaining is this: Will you continue to believe in the rope, or will you finally test your strength? Will you keep listening to the critics who say you're not enough, or will you prove to yourself, not to them that you are? Your goals, your past victories, your fears they're all part of the same story. The story of you discovering that the limitations were never real. They were simply believed. And what has been believed can be changed. The hidden power is yours. It always has been.

## Reflection Questions:

1. What are your primary goals or aspirations, and how do they align with your values and passions?

_____

_____

2. What fears are keeping you from pursuing your goals?

_____

_____

3. Reflect on a specific achievement or milestone you reached despite facing skepticism or challenges from others. How did this experience shape your resilience and determination?

_____

_____

**Chapter 2**

# Life in the Valley

"Yea, though I walk through the valley of the shadow of death, I will fear no evil." Ps 23:4

**Entry into the Valley**

Life is impersonal, but so many people take their experiences personally. Few people understand the concept that life is not happening to you, it is happening for you. As I write this book, it is my continued hope to help others see they are not alone. The experiences of life can easily steal your joy when you believe them to be painful and unbearable.

As children we are labeled and categorized according to our successes, failures, and behaviors. These labels are given to us by parents, family members, teachers, and peers. Unfortunately, in our lack of understanding as children, we tend to accept these labels. They follow us through life and determine our decisions in many aspects of life. When you believe the negative opinions, you will act upon those beliefs.

Growing up, I was an average student at best. In grade school, I was placed in remedial reading and math because of my grades. It was said I was a slow learner. Our self-esteem and beliefs about who we are can be traced back to these labels. You may have received poor grades in various school subjects and were told you are either a slow learner or incapable of understanding.

"As a man thinketh in his heart, so is he." Proverbs 23:7

Not knowing who we are growing up is a common issue for everyone. Insecurities ruled a great number of my decisions. Fearing to take chances, fear of asking women for a date, fear of pursuing the things I desired most, is how I lived. This is not how most people see me.

There are two reasons I enlisted in the military. It was instilled in me that serving is an honorable thing to do. Listening to my grandfather's stories of his experiences in World War II inspired me with the desire to serve. The other reason for me to enlist is one which is seldom revealed until recently. It was my way of running away from home. My ticket to get out of my hometown. The feeling of not being loved or part of the family was embedded in my thoughts.

The military presented a great number of opportunities which strengthened my confidence. No one knew who I was, and many accepted me into the mix. Despite the successes, insecurities lingered in the background just like the programs which run in the background on your computer or cell phone. This is an issue for each of us. Few people understand this concept about our internal programming. It took most of my life to discover this as a hindrance. The successes I experienced in the military did not follow me, nor was I able to translate them in the civilian sector.

The habit of blaming others for my emotional state of mind, the lack of success, and the lack of healthy relationships had me spiraling downwards. Like most people, I believed being married would make me feel complete. Finding the perfect employer was a goal in pursuit of happiness and success. Neither makes for a sound philosophy of life. Both are detrimental to a healthy state of being.

Marriage did not bring me happiness. Earning a decent wage was not the answer. Neither was any of the choices I made in regard to employers. One of my closest friends told me over lunch recently how I came across. They said, "You seemed angry and lost." They hit the mark with this observation. Going to work and going home from work were equally miserable for me.

My wife and coworkers kept telling me I needed to change to accommodate their feelings. They were both right and wrong on this subject. In 2020 I felt as if I had hit rock bottom. Going through divorce, battling cancer, dealing with periods of unemployment, and a second unfulfilling relationship took their toll. The employer I was working for at the time was of little help. No one in my circle understood where I was coming from, nor could they relate.

**The Shadow of Death**

And the Lord God said, "It is not good that man should be alone." Genesis 2:18

In early November 2020 I was sitting at the kitchen table. The weather outside was beautiful and the sun was shining through the windows lighting up my home. My focus was on my studies and the inspiring article which was before me. The kitchen table is cluttered with papers and books. My laptop is open, and YouTube is playing for noise in the background.

My pets, Scout and Spike are laying a few steps away, as they are patiently waiting for some attention.

A disturbing thought breaks in to disrupt my focus. It speaks calmly and softly as though to comfort my soul. "It would be so easy. You have guns, they are close by, and no one is around. You have a beautiful home, a big backyard to cookout. No one comes to visit. No one calls to check on you or to talk. It has been weeks since you last spoke to your friends or family. Do they really care?"

I recall an article of a veteran who passed a few months earlier. The article tells of how this person had been dead for three to four months before anyone thought to check on them. It says they had no family or friends to claim them. No one to come by to visit on a regular basis. There was public support from complete strangers for this person in attending their funeral.

This scenario continued to play out. Scout and Spike would need to eat. How do they have access to food, so I am not their lunch? What would be the best way to feed them? Scout will need to go outside so he does not make a mess in the house. Spike has a litter box which needs to be cleaned. What do I do? How long will it be before someone thinks to come by or to check on me? Who will come? What will happen to Scout and Spike? Will they be alive when I am found? If so, what will happen to them? Will they be adopted by someone new? They cannot speak for themselves.

The next thought was the answer which caused a change in my thinking. If they are still alive, they could very well be euthanized. Both are rescue pets and this was the reason they were adopted. They are both intelligent and deserving of a good home. In rescuing them from death, I rescued myself from suicide. Tears streaming down my face in knowing, "It would not be so easy."

58,220 is reported as the death toll of U.S. troops from the Vietnam War. The U.S. started sending troops in 1960 and pulled out in 1977. There was a recent article I saw on LinkedIn which stated that the suicide death toll of U.S. veterans of the past ten years has surpassed the Vietnam death toll. Whether it is by one or one thousand, this is alarming. It is understandable that casualties are part of battle and war. Unfortunately, it is the battle in the mind which goes undetected.

Suicide is not a solution for any problem. Instead, it opens up a great number of other problems and leaves family and friends in turmoil, sorrow, and with a wealth of unanswered questions.

**Finding Your "Why"**

Scout and Spike are my reason "Why." Why giving up is not an option. What is my purpose in life? What can I do in pursuit of my dream?

Every day is a gift which is why you have been awakened. What are the gifts you possess? What is your purpose? One thing I can promise! The creator of the universe is not holding the strings and using you as a plaything for their amusement.

You are not entertaining the creator through your trials, challenges, and adversity. What kind of cruelty is it to cause another to trip and fall for amusement?

The answer is different for each person. It is the uniqueness you possess. What are your reasons for your happiness? How do you keep your thoughts on hope? The idea of fulfillment as you walk on life's journey lie within you.

## Learning to Walk Through the Valley

This is how I came to personal development. For once in my life, I determined to do something for myself. This was completely out of character for me. However, it was the best decision for my state of mind. Making this decision came about after completing a Tony Robbins seminar. It was at this point where I realized I needed to take a new path. This is where my mentor found me.

In working with my mentor, they taught me being vulnerable is not weakness, it is strength. Boys are taught it is not manly to cry. Though many men do cry. Imagine a steam cooker if it is prevented from venting will explode. The same holds true for a person. This is why people will experience a nervous breakdown. Our thoughts are an energy which are constantly flowing.

Unguarded thoughts will take you places which are not enjoyable. How many people suffer because of the beliefs they possess about themselves and the world around them? "Keep your heart with all diligence, for out of it spring the issues of life." Proverbs 4:23 Learning to keep control of our thoughts is not something we are taught. We are told, calm down, take it easy, or don't get mad with no explanation on how or why.

The major life changes and experiences were not as problematic or the cause of my depression. Cancer, divorce, career change, and unemployment is not uncommon in life. The biggest problems are the unguarded thoughts frequently entertained as well as suppressing ourselves in avoiding confrontation. Emotions are to be expressed and not suppressed.

Holding onto grudges became a habit for me. Wanting to express exactly what I was thinking would have detrimental consequences both at home and at work. It is a lonely experience not having someone to relate to or speak to about the difficulties in life.

What both my mentor and the materials I study taught me is a new way to think. There are lessons to learn from adversity. Pursuing a goal, living for what you desire, and focus on improving yourself. Each experience requires change, it is part of growth.

In the military we always had something to aim for. Pursuing advancements, qualifications, and a wealth of study and training was our life. The lack of goals causes a great number of problems and limits our abilities to succeed. Goals are those things which we pursue. They allow us to grow, to gain confidence in understanding more about ourselves. This is what I have come to learn after being introduced to the world of personal development.

Depression can be a tool for a greater understanding of who you are. It is not a place where you want to be or a place to test your metal. Through studying I came to realize suicide is not a solution or option for a temporary problem. What is left in the wake of a suicide are the broken hearts of family and friends. Questions overcome them along with guilt.

## Reflection Questions:

1. Describe a time when you felt like you were "in the valley." What kept you walking through instead of staying stuck?

   _____

   _____

2. Who or what is your "Scout and Spike", your reason why giving up is not an option?

   _____

   _____

3. What unguarded thoughts do you need to gain control over?

   _____

   _____

4. Practice: Write down one emotion you've been suppressing and allow yourself to feel it fully.

   _____

   _____

## Chapter 3

# Tapping into the Power Within

"Ask, and it will be given to you; seek, and you will find; knock, and it will be opened to you." Mattew 7:7

**The Power Is Already Within You**

"Nowhere has it been written that circumstance has dominion over man." This is one of the most profound statements I read some time ago. It is written that God has given dominion to man over all things.

Every day you wake up with dreams, desires, and ideas inside you. The house you live in, the electronic devices you use, your automobile were all conceived in someone's imagination. This someone had a vision, put it to paper, then made definite plans for its creation. Where do these ideas come from? They come from within.

When you read from the book of Genesis in the Bible, the formation of the earth was birthed in thought, then spoken into existence. The words you speak, the movement of your body, what you believe comes from thought. Your emotions are determined by your thoughts as well. Where do your thoughts come from? Why is this important to know? Not everything you see or hear is true.

"Everything you hear is an opinion, not a fact. Everything you see is a perspective, not the truth." Marcus Aurelius, Roman Emperor

Imagination has a great impact on both success and failure. "What man can conceive in his mind, he can achieve." Napoleon Hill. Understanding we each have a dream to pursue is where the power is. The power is within. Looking inward and identifying what you truly desire is the first step.

**Bringing It to Light**

This is how my mentor helped me. They listened, took the time to understand, and offered a perspective to bring out something positive. Coupled with bringing our deep-seated pain to the surface. What is made light is made manifest, and something which can be addressed and corrected.

Being around people who are supportive, uplifting, and non-judgmental can help with problem solving and understanding. My mentor did not give me power. They helped me tap into the power that was already there. This is what happens when you create the right environment to look inward.

The tension and resistance will block the chances for success. Thoughts and ideas are difficult to come by when your mind is filled with worries, stress, and tension. Your mind can only hold one thought at a time. Holding onto a past hurt, disappointment, or problem causes the resistance. This is the biggest reason most people struggle with meditation.

Your mind and your thoughts are energy which is constantly flowing. This concept may sound strange for many people. It was difficult for me to grasp at first as it was easier to think of other people as the cause of my problems. This is how most people are conditioned to believe. How often have you blamed someone else for your feelings of anger, sadness, disappointment?

Even your emotions of joy, happiness, and laughter are attributed to what others may say or do. Your emotions are internal and are determined by your values, beliefs, and thoughts you entertain. One particular evening I happened to be listening to Dr. Wayne Dyer on the subject of emotions. He used the analogy of the orange. "What do you get when you squeeze an orange?" Orange juice.

The juice is already inside the orange. You did not put it inside in order for it to come out. Anger, happiness, joy, sadness, and all of the other emotions are inside you. They are not connected to any outside source which causes you to feel these emotions.

**You Cannot Do It Alone**

It is written, when two or more come together in prayer to the Lord in agreement it will be given. There is an entrepreneurial concept referred to as a mastermind. What does this mean? When you are in alliance with two or more people in the spirit of harmony, your chances of success are greater than if you worked alone. Prayer is a harmonious form of communication in seeking the noble desires of your heart.

Your chances of getting what you desire is increased when you ask for help or guidance. No successful individual achieved their goals by working alone. Thomas Edison, Henry Ford, Bob Proctor, Earl Nightingale, and several other successful individuals utilized the concept of the mastermind, meditation, in search for answers in reaching their goals. There are many people who attend church services seeking help through prayer.

The concept of masterminding is when two or more people put their collective minds together to help one another in overcoming obstacles and achieving goals. My mentor introduced me to this concept through the teachings of Bob Proctor. This process was taught to Bob by his mentors and from the book Think and Grow Rich, written by Napoleon Hill.

Harmony is the key component. Not everyone who you know or meet are going to cheer you along or help you. This is a simple fact of life. This is why each of us seek one or two people who we can confide in with the issues of life. What is meant by harmony is, there is no resistance, no tension involved.

As I stated earlier, not everyone whom you know will be cheering you on for success. It is unfortunate that those who are closest to you will be against you. This is important to know because it is my hope that you find the people who are willing to lift you up for success.

When you consider your friends there are those who lift you up and those who will hold you accountable. Then there are those who will drag you down. This is a simple fact of life. Never choose your friends who involve themselves with gossip and discord. It has been a proven fact that states your habits are similar to the people you hang around with. This is important to know when going through the process to mastermind.

As I have learned, sharing your dreams with too many people hinders you in their pursuit. Another person who has influenced me is a notable author from the 1930s. One of the things they stated when you share your dreams with too many people, you dissipate your energy for your success.

It is written in the Bible to seek wisdom and understanding. Surrounding yourself with people who seek a noble purpose will often take you further than a college degree. There is a Bible verse which says iron sharpens iron. Taken into consideration, you must have something to offer in fair trade with the people you spend time with.

**Opening Yourself to Receive**

When you are in harmony, you surrender and release the tension which will prevent the flow of ideas and inspired thoughts. Belief is just as important as harmony. If you do not believe your prayers are answered or what members of your mastermind group are sharing, you will not receive what you are seeking. When a loved one, a friend, or a stranger come up to ask you for help, they believe you have the ability to help.

"If you can believe, all things are possible to him who believes." Mark 9:23

How do you go about the process of masterminding? Taking the time to ask questions and research the process will move you in the right direction. Success is a process to study, to learn, and put into practice. There is a science to becoming wealthy. The number of success books are readily available yet oftentimes missed because people are too busy with trivial activities.

This is one area I wish I would have known years ago. Too many people struggle through the process of achieving their goals. The concept of goals is seldom discussed in school, with employers, and especially within the home. This would explain why many people are financially challenged. The lack of financial education is not necessarily the problem. It is that too many people are unaware that it is available.

## Reflection Questions:

1. Write out a list of what you desire without judgment or thinking of how.

   _____

   _____

2. Ally with someone who has achieved a greater level of success than you.

   _____

   _____

3. Open yourself to receive coaching and knowledge.

   _____

   _____

# Chapter 4

# Forgiveness

"Forgive us our trespasses as we forgive those who trespass against us." Matthew 6:12

### What Is Forgiveness?

Forgiveness is the first step to healing. What is forgiveness? You are told to forgive but no one explains the concept. In studying the Bible, it is written in the Lord's prayer. "Forgive us our trespasses as we forgive those who trespass against us." The concept is in reference to sowing and reaping. There are universal laws which apply equally to each of us. The Law of Cause and Effect, the Law of Vibration, the Law of Attraction to name a few. You will always receive what you give whether it is good or bad.

Life is impersonal, yet we make it personal. It is the lack of forgiveness which causes the greatest pain. As defined in Webster's New World Dictionary and Thesaurus, to forgive is to give up resentment against or the desire to punish, pardon an offense or offender. To break it down further, to forgive is to let go of the mental bondage between you and the offender or offense. In general, people hold grudges, resentment, and bitterness long after a painful experience.

Imagine a rose stem. The roses are very beautiful and captivating. If you are careless in grabbing the stem, you will experience the sharp pain of the thorns. Even though you let it go the pain lingers for a good period. It is in the letting go which starts the healing process. Going back to the painful experiences in your life is like grabbing the rose stem again and again and again. This prolongs the healing of your heart.

When Peter asks Jesus, "How many times must I forgive my brother who sins against me? Seven times?" Jesus says, "No! Seventy times seven." Think of the number of times you asked for forgiveness. If you have not asked for forgiveness, you may not have been forgiven. Forgiveness sets you free from the mental bondage to the person or the offense which caused the pain, the disappointment, or the loss. Forgiveness is a practice not because you must. Instead, it is because this is the right thing to do.

Forgiveness is for you, not the offense or the offender. Forgiveness is a daily practice which opens you up to receive greater fulfillment and joy. There is no prosperity in life without forgiveness. As you forgive, never neglect to forgive yourself.

## Forgiving Your Family

Our first experiences in relationships begins in childhood with our immediate family. Our esteem is gifted to us by our parents as we grow up. Family curses have been the topic of some discussions over the past couple of years. The addictions, health issues, and the family dynamics we observe firsthand.

What we each believe about ourselves has been determined by a family member who may have said something which was painful or demeaning. As I have come to learn, no one likes to be criticized or to be told they are not good enough. Children are no exception.

We are dependent on our parents for a great number of things. Esteem is one of them. We seek acknowledgement, encouragement, and validation from our parents or an adult who we admire. Unfortunately, most adults are expecting children to think and act like adults. We are admonished for whatever mistakes we make such as crawling on the floor getting our clothes dirty or for having a messy room. For those fortunate or unfortunate to have siblings, the feeling of competition for recognition comes into existence.

The concept of "middle child syndrome" is a term I heard a few years ago. This is the child who is bracketed by an older and younger sibling. Both the elder and younger siblings are praised and acknowledged for their accomplishments while the middle child seems to go unnoticed until they do something wrong. This is what I experienced. This left the feeling of being left out, or not good enough because the mistakes are amplified with harsh words. Children do not know how to frame their thoughts or manage their emotions.

This causes our insecurities to follow us into adulthood. There are those who deal with the inferiority complex and some with the superiority complex. Both are reflections of childhood scars of criticism, judgement, and the feelings of being ignored. There are many people who are told by a parent that they are not good enough or that they will not amount to anything. This is a painful experience for a child because of our innocence and childhood ignorance. Children have a greater understanding of love than most adults. They seemingly have the inherent ability to forgive despite the harshness of a parent's admonishment.

Coming from a single parent home leaves a great void in our hearts. There are a number of studies which have demonstrated that children who come from a two-parent home tend to experience greater levels of success and a more balanced life. There is contrast and comparison between the mother and father. Each of them represents both a positive and negative example for children. Observing my father, he was heavy handed in his admonishments. My mother was as well. As I have matured, both did possess a loving concern for my siblings and myself.

**Forgiving Yourself**

How is this a thing? Feelings of guilt and shame for something you have done or what you are currently doing. Pornography, gambling, infidelity, drugs, and alcohol use bring these feelings. These vices hinder a great number of people in various ways. These vices steal your time, money, and opportunities to have healthy relationships and an abundant life.

Long before I was old enough for marriage, I knew what kind of man I wanted to be. Being a loving husband and father is a dream of mine. Wanting to be remembered for the good things and not the bad things you do can weigh heavy on your mind. No one I have met tell of their dreams of being hated or resented after they are gone. This one reason for forgiveness. To set you free from the bondage of bitterness.

We judge ourselves for failing to live according to our principles. Being unfaithful in my marriage is not something to be proud of. Just because it is a common issue in society does not make it right. Regardless of the things your spouse may do or not do, infidelity only adds to the problems in marriage. As I graded myself, guilt and shame are the things I hid from family and friends. It is a heavy burden to carry.

I have done several things in the past which I am not proud of, yet, knowing they cannot be undone, changed, or erased, holding onto the guilt and shame is more damaging to your body than you know. There have been medical and scientific studies of how our emotions impact our physical health. Think of the how many people contend with peptic ulcers, muscle tension, and headaches because of stress, worry, and anger.

There is a wealth of information which gives clarity and understanding regarding our thoughts. I learned that our pet peeves are more often the bad habits we possess. In judging and criticizing others, it is an unconscious behavior in trying to hide our own mistakes. Getting the attention of parents, teachers, managers, and other authority figures to look at someone else's mistake rather than our own keeps us safe for a short while.

This is the blame game we learn as children. Your mother or father asks, "Who did that?" The responses are comical now, "I don't know" "It was like that when I came inside." Or we point the finger at a sibling or friend. Now we are known as a "snitch." Asking for forgiveness by admitting our mistakes is easier if not for the fear of punishment.

Judging others is a way to deflect and avoid offering forgiveness.

## Forgiving Those Who Hurt You

My lack of forgiveness gave me sleepless nights over the years. It caused an overabundance of stress, resentment, and missed opportunities for advancement both in the military and civilian sectors. It impacted personal and professional relationships. Holding onto the pain, the anger, the bitterness is like consuming a steady dose of poison and expecting the other person to suffer or die. The other person may not be aware of your resentment and are happy to move along.

Anger is permitted and understandable according to the written word. Holding onto it is not. Aside from the missed opportunities, conflicts, and sleepless nights, the lack of forgiveness kept me from God's grace. How could He forgive me when I did not forgive? How could you expect a blessing, something new while holding onto the old experience? Everything in life is temporary. You are not happy, sad, angry, or hungry 100 percent of the time. Each passing moment brings new thoughts, new experiences, and each are just for a moment in time. It is when you hold onto one thought, one bad experience. This is what causes the suffering.

Back in 2002 as I was reading the Bible, I got to a part which talks about forgiveness. I remember crying, realizing that I had been so selfish. Knowing now that the lack of forgiveness is a heavy burden to carry. Earnestly, I offered a wealth of forgiveness to so many people which I learned to despise for one reason or another.

It was a dark night, even darker in my room because the moon was hidden. As I laid down to sleep, I closed my eyes and remember being enveloped by this bright light. Quickly, I opened my eyes and saw darkness. Closing them brought this bright light which surrounded me. It seemed to swallow me as it moved upwards over my head. It is difficult to explain this experience in detail except to say it lasted until I fell asleep.

When I woke up the following morning, it felt as if an enormous weight had been lifted off my shoulders. I felt rested, refreshed, and a sense of peace. All the anger, resentment, disappointments, and the feelings of rejection no longer seemed to exist. I remember how quick I was to lose my temper and how I really didn't like myself. I didn't want to be around me and can only imagine no one else wanted too either.

Forgiveness is something to learn, to understand as it will set you free from the burdens you are carrying. Learning not to be attached to the things people may say or do towards you is liberating. How many relationships could be salvaged or saved by learning how to forgive?

Rejection is a blessing in disguise. Those who don't want to spend time with you are doing you an enormous favor. You are free from giving time and energy to someone who may judge or speak poorly of you. Bless them, walk away free from worry. They are not your crowd. Those who accept you are not hung up on the things you may say or do. They will listen to what you say, they will guide you on a path which brings growth. This took me years to learn. If you remember one simple thing, not everyone Loved Jesus. Why would you expect anything different?

Be honest about this as well. Do you like everyone who you meet? This is how I have come to see this. Each of us vibrate on frequencies. This has given new meaning to the concept of "Birds of a feather flock together." You spend more time with people who think more like you.

## The Daily Practice of Forgiveness

The Law of Vibration is one of many universal laws which applies to everything. The vibrations are frequencies. Light, sound, bodies, and all of nature are based on frequencies. The sound of my voice as I speak is on a specific frequency. This sound is picked up by your ears, goes down your ear canal to the middle ear, the three small bones vibrate based on the frequency, then send an electric signal to your brain and what I said is then interpreted by your brain. You assign a specific value to what I say based on several variable factors.

If you and I are communicating on the right frequency, we may come to know one another as friends. If not, the chances are we will not spend any energy communicating in the future. Imagine the radio, it receives several incoming frequencies based on the dial selection. Whatever frequency you are dialed into is what you will receive. If you are listening to an FM radio station, you will not receive anything transmitting on an AM radio station.

Understanding your emotions have their own frequencies helps to know when you are angry, you are probably annoyed when someone who is cheerful enters the room. You and the people around you are not always on the same frequency. Knowing this will help you as you go through the day and will allow you to forgive others who are not operating on your frequency.

I was listening to a pastor not long ago talk about forgiveness. It was an amazing sermon, and one point in particular, left an impact on me. Quite simply, before you can forgive another person, you first must condemn them. This made me think. Have I condemned those individuals in the past for the wrongs which they imposed upon me? Is it the ignorance about forgiveness holding anyone back from receiving the abundance which we desire?

Forgiveness is not carnal. It is however spoken on the physical plane. It allows for both mental and spiritual healing. Always remember our time on earth is temporary. To live in harmony with others is to forgive one another at all times. This is what sets you free from those who have caused you pain. We are instructed to agree with our enemies as well, to love our enemies. This is contrary to what we learn on a personal level.

Forgiveness is how we continually receive forgiveness from God. Life is about sowing and reaping in all areas of life. Earning an income, establishing friendships, improving the results we receive is based on our own efforts in giving.

Colossians 3:12 – "If anyone has a complaint against another, even as Christ forgave you, so you also must do."

# Reflection Questions:

1. What are your beliefs about forgiveness?

_____

_____

2. Have you forgiven yourself?

_____

_____

3. Are you holding onto an experience where you have not forgiven another?

_____

_____

## Chapter 5

# A Grateful Heart

Gratitude has been attributed for the success of those who have gained prosperity. With all that is going on in the world, in your life good or bad, there is always something to be grateful for. There are many who feel their world is crashing down on them with their finances, relationships, and job but always seem to smile. There are others with the same experiences walking around with bitterness and a lack of hope.

What is the difference between the two? Their perspective, their attitude, and their beliefs. There is so much to be grateful for but so many people miss it. The opportunity to travel around the world visiting third world countries has given me a perspective which faded over the years. Knowing there are people in the world who do not possess the luxuries we often take for granted here in America.

This is not to say everyone in America have the luxury of a home with air conditioning or heat. When you have never had these luxuries, life has a different meaning. Having a car to take you where you want to go, a warm bed to sleep in during the winter. This could be a long list to write out. Despite these luxuries and opportunities there are so many people who are miserable with their lives.

For some reason we have become caught up in looking for external sources of joy, happiness, and fulfillment. Being bombarded with advertisements of products which are promoted as must haves is overwhelming. Think about how your garage is packed with possessions which have no place in your home. Your car will not fit in the garage because of the clutter.

What are your thoughts about these items? When is the last time you used them? Have these items brought joy into your relationships? Have they changed your perspective on the things you worry about? Material possessions like your daily thoughts serve a temporary purpose. Like your thoughts of bad experiences, you still hold onto them.

When is the last time you looked at your spouse with love and gratitude? Did you marry them because of the money they earn or the things they possess? We have each paid for a mistake many times over because of the habit of holding onto pain and disappointment. What would your relationship look like if you were to focus on the good things over the bad?

Adversity is part of life, and no one is exempt in this area. Think of all of your past experiences good and bad. Do an inventory of what you learned from the adversity. Did you learn more from the adversity or from the easy times? We are taught once again in the Bible to approach prayer with a glad heart.

Do you have a better day at work and with your family when you are in a good mood? Do you feel better about yourself when you are able to help a stranger or a family member? Being grateful along with forgiveness is more uplifting than bitterness and resentment. The unfortunate thing is habitually holding onto bad experiences.

In June and July of 2020, I attended two Tony Robbins seminars. This is where the concept of gratitude was brought to my attention. Though I attended hundreds of church services and parties, the concept of gratitude had eluded me. Feelings of bitterness, anger, resentment, and unforgiveness still ruled my life. Learning about forgiveness and gratitude gave me a new perspective on life.

Life is in a constant state of change. Everything is temporary and serves a purpose for a period of time. You literally get a new body every eighteen months. Everything in nature goes through a period of growth and change. Gratitude is in accepting and appreciating the things you have and which you may receive. Forgiveness is letting go of the past. Both are gifts you possess and will bring you a greater level of joy.

Being grateful for a new day with new opportunities brings even more to be grateful for. There are lessons to be learned in adversity regardless of the circumstances. Looking for the lesson will give you more insight to who you are. The joys you experience in life begin with you. There were a few people I know who asked me about writing a book.

For me, talking about my life did not seem so interesting. The people who are now friends would have never entered my life without the practices I want to share with you. The people in the past who I was in conflict with are in the past. When you think of how trees shed their leaves in autumn, remember you drop people and experiences as you grow in life.

**Philippians 4:8**

Finally, brethren, whatever things are true, whatever things are noble, whatever things are just, whatever things are pure, whatever things are lovely, whatever things are of good report, if there is any virtue and if there is anything praiseworthy – meditate on these things.

This scripture is worth learning and keeping on the forefront of your thinking. There are a number of Bible scriptures which bring hope and comfort during trials and adversity. It may sound easier said than done. You are the one who has power over the thoughts you entertain. Keeping your mind on the good is not as tiring as focusing on the negative.

Years ago, I experienced one of the most disappointing failures while attending an electrical school in the Navy. Failing a test on troubleshooting an electrical circuit when I was confident of the answer. This failure caused me to fail an entire week of study where I maintained a GPA of 4.0. The repercussion was to be placed in the class one week behind in the school.

My anger and frustration carried throughout the day. It was something I could not let go of. When school was dismissed at 3:00 p.m., I went straight to sleep in my bunk. I was mentally and physically exhausted. It was 5:00 a.m. the next morning when I woke up. This experience of anger caused me to miss the evening meal and the evening study time.

Suppressing my feelings about this failure was not a healthy thing to do. Not expressing your thoughts and emotions are taxing on your health, mentally, physically, and spiritually. This is what experience has taught me. It is a high price to pay and one many people suffer from. Opportunities are missed when the focus is on problems over solutions.

For years, I held onto the anger from that failure. I couldn't see any lesson in it, only injustice. What I didn't understand then was that my lack of forgiveness—toward myself, toward the situation, toward the instructor who graded that test—kept me anchored to that moment. It minimized any gratitude I could have felt for the opportunities I still had. The Bible teaches us to forgive before we pray to God. It's like washing your hands before you sit down to eat. Forgiveness strengthens and lightens you, preparing your heart to express gratitude and receive something new. Without forgiveness, gratitude struggles to take root.

Those who maintain poise and calm in the face of adversity experience greater success.

The practice of gratitude is something we are not taught growing up. Someone may say, "Be grateful for what you have." They don't explain as to why. What I learned from Tony Robbins, my mentor, and how practicing gratitude is transformative. It shifts your mind, your thoughts, and energy to joy, happiness, and a certain sense of peace that you are blessed.

What I learned about the practice of gratitude and forgiveness is both give you strength and confidence. They change your perspective about life and the people around you. Personal development has transformed my life exponentially and it has helped to open doors for new opportunities. Opportunities which I never once imagined.

It is humbling when people ask for your perspective, they invite you to new opportunities. For example, the friend who introduced me to the publisher of this book. I believe, if my attitude was negative, confrontational, and I spent time complaining, this opportunity would have never come to be.

Gratitude and forgiveness when combined will not only set you free from the past, but also opens you up to receive the blessings and opportunities you deserve.

So, here's what I'm asking you to do. Not because it sounds nice, but because it works. Start today. Right now, identify three things you're grateful for. Don't overthink it—your health, your family, the roof over your head, the ability to read these words. Feel that shift happening inside you as you name them. That feeling? That's your perspective changing in real time. Now imagine doing this every single morning for 30 days. Imagine starting each day from that place of abundance instead of lack, gratitude instead of complaint. The transformation isn't theory—it's inevitable.

## Reflection Questions:

1. List three things that you are grateful for.

_____

_____

2. What experiences are you grateful for today?

_____

_____

3. Practice the concept of daily gratitude to start your day for 30 days.

_____

_____

4. Close your eyes and picture in your mind someone or something that brings you joy. Smile and say, "I am grateful for." Then write down how you feel about this new practice.

_____

_____

## Chapter 6

# Write Your Own Story

A common teaching in church and certain circles we are taught God spoke the world into existence. This is true but what most people have not stated. God thought the world and the universe into existence before He spoke it into existence. This can be referenced in the book of Genesis. We are taught God created man in His own image. He has gifted each of us with creative abilities and an amazing imagination. Your dreams often reflect what you imagine.

Have you ever wondered where your dreams originate? How can you see vivid images in your dreams to where when you wake up and wonder if the dream was real? Think back to when you were a child, and you drew pictures with just your imagination. Do you remember making up songs to sing to your parents? No one had taught you how to write music or lyrics, but yet you were singing. This is how your amazing mind works without much effort on your part.

There are a great number of people who are living the life they desire. They are earning the money they desire, traveling around the world, learning new things. Then there are those who are living in poverty, moving from job to job, from one relationship to another. What is the difference? Opportunity? Education? Money? It is the environment they are living in, to a certain degree.

As I study success and successful people, the great majority of them come from humble beginnings. Steve Harvey, Bob Proctor, Earl Nightingale, Andrew Carnegie, Cristiano Ronaldo, are examples of people coming out of poverty to living an abundant life. Some of these individuals were introduced to a mentor, some pursued their dreams with all they had inside. Their success did not come easy or without failure.

You are the author of your life the opportunities that you have when you wake up each day are limitless. It isn't the lack of time or the lack of money which is the problem it is your perception of the lack of both. We each get 24 hours a day to do the things we believe we must do. Many people with whom I have met say, if I don't write it on the calendar it doesn't happen. When you understand the calendar is to write important activities and scheduling events, you can use it to schedule time for yourself.

Scheduling time to exercise, read a book, or take a class to learn a new skill is an opportunity which people pass up. The decisions you make in life are yours alone. When you have a vision to pursue a particular goal or a dream it isn't there by accident. When you take the time to write down your dream it becomes a goal.

Most people see the challenges of time and money as reasons not to pursue their dreams. The reason for writing out your goals is that it gives your mind an aiming point. A direction to take towards the destination. Close your eyes and imagine what this looks like, how you feel when you have achieved the goal. In chapter 3, I talked about the power within. This is where your dreams come from. They have been gifted to you.

Written in Habakkuk 2:2 in the Bible, it gives an instruction on how to write out your dream. To put it into detail as if you are able to give it to someone else and they would be able to create this dream. It is clear, and understood. Time and money are not the problem as much as fear, doubt, and a negative belief.

When people write out a deadline or date to reach their goal, it creates not only a sense of urgency. It also allows for ideas to come into your thoughts, an inspiration to act upon as you progress towards your goal. It further gives you a purpose and action items to reduce procrastination and stagnation.

When you imagine your goal, you can ask what can I do to make this happen? You can then brainstorm to come up with ideas and action items to move you towards this goal.

When you put this into action this becomes your To Do List. This is one method which you can use to overcome procrastination. It has been determined that only 3% of the population have their goals written down and clearly defined. The rest of the population goes from day-to-day with no particular direction. This is the biggest reason so many people are unfulfilled in their life. When you have no specific direction to move towards it is easy to become lost.

In 2003 after I separated from the Navy, I didn't have any goals. I had an idea of what I wanted but was halfhearted in my efforts. My reason for a lack of success was based on the idea that I lacked education, experience, and not knowing the right people. As I have learned this is a common alibi for the millions of people who are unhappy with their lives. When you have no direction, it is also easy to become discouraged.

Happiness isn't something you receive it is something you create. When you are doing the things which bring pleasure to your life you are more energized, excited, and more productive in your daily activities. When you worry about the things you don't have you miss out on the opportunities to achieve the things you want. When you understand the concept of contentment, you become aware of the gratitude for what you have.

As I have come to learn gratitude is a principle put into practice by those who are achieving their goals. When you practice gratitude, you increase your vibration level to a more positive level which will attract more opportunities which take you towards your goal. Do not concern yourself with how to achieve your goal if you knew how you would already be there.

Seeking a mentor who has already achieved what you desire is a positive step in the right direction. Having a mentor can cut down the time necessary in achieving your goals. It has been my experience those who desire to mentor do so out of compassion and understanding. Mentors are those who love to share the principles of success with those individuals committed to themselves. This is important to know because too many people seek the validation of others.

Your confidence level will increase when you see the progress you are making in achieving your goal. Those who have acquired great wealth have said, "it isn't what you achieve but who you become when you achieve your goal." Working towards a goal will cause you greater satisfaction and growth. What is growth you may ask. It is becoming whom you were created to be.

You are not created to merely exist, just to pay taxes, or to be miserable. Each of us have a purpose to fulfill. This is why the dreams we have are placed on our heart. It would be cruel for the creator to find pleasure in the suffering of their creation. Waking up in the morning knowing the direction you're to go, will give you something to look forward to.

Now it's time for you to create your world. The reflection points below are not just questions—they are your opportunity to dream without limits. Close your eyes. Let go of time and money. What do you see?

## Reflection Questions:

1. Do you have a goal you desire to achieve?

2. Do you have it written down?

3. Do you have a deadline to accomplish it?

4. If time and money were not an issue, what would you pursue?

## Chapter 7

# Unconditional Love

Love never fails. 1 Corinthians 13:8

What is love? Love is not physical, it is spiritual, it is resonance, it is harmony. All too often, we love with conditions. When people are doing what we desire, there are thoughts of love. As soon as they are doing the opposite of what is expected, there is friction, feelings of confusion. Why are they causing this pain?

We each have our values, beliefs, and desires. It is easy to love when the people close to us are doing what we desire. This is the harmony, the resonance, this is what fills us with a sense of joy. When people are going against what we expect or desire, there is friction, our hearts are out of alignment. We feel a sense of anger, disappointment, and confusion.

When we persist in our expectations, this adds to our frustrations. A few years ago, I met a woman through a networking group who later became a dear friend. Originally there seemed to be uncertainty as to whether there was an opportunity to work together. There were mixed signals from my perspective based on her body language. Over time, we became good friends, and I would say she is someone I came to love.

What made this special for me is that she taught me a lot about how to listen. Prior to meeting her, I had prayed for my ideal partner, the woman who I would want to marry. As I prayed, there was a list of qualities and characteristics which are both attractive and desirable for me. There was no face, name, or image of any woman, just the qualities.

In listening to her when we met for a social event, I learned that she possesses a great number of the qualities and characteristics which I prayed about. Feeling comfortable with my ideal partner is one of the qualities I prayed for. I believe we are all looking for that special someone with whom we can just be and feel content with who we are. No judgement, no awkward feelings, and you just like who you are.

What I learned from this experience is that recognizing the qualities you desire does not guarantee the relationship you hope for. She possessed everything I prayed for, yet we were not meant to be together romantically. At first, this felt like a cruel joke—why would God show me exactly what I wanted, only to keep it out of reach? But the lesson became clear over time: she was not sent to be my partner.

She was sent to show me that the qualities I prayed for actually exist, and to prepare my heart to recognize them when the right person arrives. She was a teacher, not the destination. Sometimes people come into our lives to show us what is possible, to raise our standards, to prove we are not asking for too much. Their departure does not mean our prayer was wrong—it means we are being prepared for what is coming.

She was involved with another man, and I had thought how fortunate he was. Eventually, that relationship ended, leaving her with heartbreak and confusion. This is something we can all relate to. The pain of losing the person we love. This brings me back to the question, "What is love?"

Love is not what you find in other people, instead it is a seed you plant by giving of yourself. Think about what this truly means. A farmer plants seeds not knowing if the weather will cooperate, if the soil is perfect, or if every seed will produce a harvest. Yet the farmer plants anyway, trusting the process. This is how love works.

You give—your time, your attention, your care, your presence—without demanding a specific return. You plant the seed of love through your actions, your words, your compassion. Some seeds will grow into beautiful relationships. Others will not take root, and that is okay. The planting itself is the purpose.

When you love unconditionally, you are not planting seeds to possess the harvest—you are planting because that is who you are. A loving person loves, regardless of what comes back. In 1 Corinthians 13 we get an idea of what love does not do. Love does not judge, boast, or seek itself.

When you truly love, you are unattached to people, places, and things. This does not mean you do not care—it means you do not possess them. There is a profound difference between loving someone and trying to own them. Non-attachment means you love people for who they are, not for what they give you or how they make you feel. You celebrate their presence without clinging to them out of fear.

Understanding no one belongs to you and you belong to no one is not a statement of loneliness—it is where you find freedom. Every moment someone chooses to be in your life is a gift, not an obligation. It means when they leave, you cherish the time and feel content with who you are despite their absence. Honor what was shared rather than demand what you think should have been. This is the freedom that unconditional love offers.

We are all here for but a moment in time and all you experience is temporary. The friend in the previous paragraph is someone who I loved for but a moment. A few years ago, she sent me a text message on my birthday saying we can no longer be friends. Even though this was not a romantic relationship, the pain was still there.

Especially, since this occurred on my birthday. What is the lesson to learn from this? The people we love often hurt us the most. Her reasoning for the disconnection did not really make sense at the time. How do you reframe this experience?

Rejection is part of life, and it can be seen as a blessing. Her departure opens the door for the right woman to come in, the woman who is open and ready for a meaningful relationship. There was no obligation on her part to be in my life nor was I obligated. When someone walks out of your life, though it is painful, do not chase, or plead for them to stay. This sounds heartless, I am sure.

Love is unconditional, there are no strings or attachments when it comes to a friendship. Consider this, when your closest friend says or does something which may cause some pain, do you hold onto the pain? Do hold them accountable? It is often easier to forgive your best friend than it is to forgive your spouse, or the person you are romantically involved with.

What is the difference? The attachment, the expectation for a desired response. This is where we fall from grace. The expectation for a desired response. To give with expectation is troublesome.

Understanding, love is something you give as a gift, and like a birthday gift, your only desire is for the recipient to appreciate it and put it to good use. We appreciate the thank you, the look of joy, and a hug. This is something I wish someone would have taught me in my youth. That love is unconditional, and no one is obligated to be with you throughout your life.

The person who should be the primary focus of your love, is the person looking at you in the mirror. Before you can love anyone unconditionally, you must first love yourself that way. This is not selfishness—it is the foundation for life. When you love yourself without conditions, you stop criticizing every mistake, stop punishing yourself for not being perfect, and stop seeking validation from others to feel worthy. When you reflect on your past successes, the adversity you overcame, you will see not only your strength, but your value as well.

Here is what happens when you master self-love: you stop demanding conditions from others. You stop needing them to complete you, validate you, or fix you. You no longer say I will be happy when they love me back or I need them to stay for me to be okay. Instead, you realize you are whole without them. And from that wholeness, you can genuinely love others—not because you need something from them, but because you have something to give.

The person in the mirror is the one who will be with you from your first breath to your last. That person deserves your gentleness, your patience, your forgiveness, and your unwavering love. When you give that to yourself, loving others unconditionally becomes natural rather than exhausting. You are the one who gives you the biggest criticism, and the person who is going to be with you throughout your journey.

Love is tied to forgiveness, when you look at the hurt as friction. Like two pieces of metal in a gear are grinding against one another, the noise of the resistance from opposing forces. This causes heat, and eventual failure of components in machinery. When the gears are aligned, working together in unison and harmony, the machinery functions normally and produces a desired outcome. The disappointments, the hurt, and the disagreements are like the gears fighting against one another, they bring the friction.

When the gears are working together, cooperating, and moving in unison for a desired outcome, all is well. This is where we feel the love, we are in harmony with one another. Loving unconditionally does not mean you will not feel the pain when someone leaves. It means you will not let that pain turn you bitter or closed off.

The birthday text from my friend hurt—there is no denying that. But holding onto that hurt would have been worse. It would have kept me anchored to a moment that was already over, prevented me from being open to new relationships, and most importantly, it would have violated the very principle of unconditional love I am working to live by. Unconditional love requires trust.

Trust that everyone in your life is there for a reason, a season, or a lifetime—and all three are valuable. Trust that when someone walks away, it is not a rejection of your worth but a redirection toward your purpose. Trust that the right people will stay, and the wrong ones will leave, and both outcomes serve you. The question is not whether people will stay in your life.

The question is: will you keep your heart open? Will you keep loving yourself enough to let others go when it is time? Will you continue planting seeds of love even when some do not grow? This is the courage unconditional love demands.

Here is what I know now that I did not know in my youth: the greatest love you can give anyone is the freedom to be themselves and the freedom to leave. When you release expectations and attachments, you make room for authentic connection. When you love yourself first, you stop needing others to complete you. When you forgive quickly and fully, you free yourself from the prison of resentment. Love never fails—not because every relationship lasts forever, but because the act of loving transforms you into someone better.

Every person you love, even briefly, teaches you something. Every heartbreak, when processed with grace, makes you more compassionate. Every loss, when reframed, becomes an opening. So love boldly.

Love without keeping score. Love without demanding guarantees. And when love walks away, let it go with gratitude for what it taught you. Then turn to the mirror, look yourself in the eyes, and keep loving the one person who will never leave—you.

This is where unconditional love begins, and this is where it returns. Always.

## Reflection Questions:

1. Who have you been loving with conditions, and what expectations have you placed on them that create friction in the relationship?

_____

_____

2. Think of a relationship that ended painfully. What was the lesson hidden in that loss, and can you reframe the departure as an opening rather than a closing?

_____

_____

3. When you look in the mirror, what do you say to yourself? Are you giving yourself the unconditional love you desire from others?

_____

_____

4. Where are you holding onto hurt because someone did not meet your expectations? What would it feel like to forgive and let go?

_____

_____

5. If love is a seed you plant by giving, not something you find in others, what are you planting today? What are you giving without expectation of return?

_____

_____

# Chapter 8

# Your Circle Matters

There's an old cliche: "birds of a feather flock together." I never really understood it until I heard Tony Robbins say something that changed my perspective: If you want to know your future, look at the five people you hang around the most. If you spend time with people who are always negative, complaining, and criticizing, that will be your future.

As I reflected on what Tony had stated, it caused me to look inward and the choices I made about the jobs I took over the years. It seemed most people were unhappy with their jobs, their lives; they were overly critical of management and other employees. For me, it felt challenging to work with these individuals. Especially, when I found myself having to give an accounting for my efforts in performing the jobs assigned to me.

Eventually, getting up for work felt like a chore. It was no longer interesting, and my attitude had become negative as well. This is the point where you realize the honeymoon is over. Going from being excited to go to work, to dreading getting out of bed. It took me years of moving from one negative environment to another to realize that I needed to change. In September 2021, I sold my house to quit my job so I could start my own business. This was my birthday gift to me.

Years later, I discovered research that explained exactly what I had experienced. Recently, there is an influencer I follow who shared something quite interesting. They were sharing information about a study conducted to see if low performers infected the workplace. What they found is, if you sit about 25 feet from a high performer, your performance improves by fifteen percent. Consequently, if you sit 25 feet from a low performer, your performance decreases by 30 percent. Meaning, we are more easily influenced negatively rather than in a positive manner.

This brought even further reflection. What standards did I set for myself in the workplace? Was I giving my best to learn, to be productive, was I open to learning? It is also said, you attract what you are and not what you want. This is what a mentor taught me. There are so many people who want a better life but are not willing to change themselves. What a hard lesson to learn.

Your environment has a great impact on the direction of your life. To be prosperous in life, you must take the time to study and improve yourself. But here's what most people miss: you also need to surround yourself with people who are ahead of where you want to be.

Several years ago when I was stationed in Hawaii, I met a friend while playing pool at the barracks. He challenged me to a game. My pool skills were severely lacking, but I accepted, knowing he would win. As time went on, my skills improved because most of the people I played against were considerably better than me.

One day, a woman walked into the chief's club and asked about the chalkboard for the pool table. I told her she could play the winner. My friend lost to me that day—rare. I suspected this woman was a pool shark. Our first game came down to the 8 ball. From my perspective, she was going to scratch and lose. She made the 8 ball in the pocket she called without coming close to scratching. The games that followed, she won easily, leaving me with two to three balls on the table. After a while, she admitted to being a tournament player.

I have never been one to give up, and I believed that I would win against this woman. Of course, I couldn't help but laugh when she revealed the truth about being a tournament player. She did commend me for the persistence in trying to win. There was no shame in losing against a woman, especially, if she is a professional player.

What I learned: if you want to succeed at anything in life, surround yourself with people who are better than you. If you want to be successful in business, learn from those who are doing what you want to do. This will shave years of heartache and struggles. Most of the people I spend time with are more than willing to help or share knowledge. One big change I made aside from quitting my job was to walk away from the negative people on social media as well. This has had a major impact on both my mindset and overall outlook on life.

The best people to spend time with are those who lift you up, encourage you, and are willing to share their knowledge with you. When you look for the good in others, you often discover the good in yourself.

One principle keeps showing itself to me: you will always reap what you sow. If you sow negative thoughts, your results will be negative. Life is about growing, improving, and learning new skills. The more you focus on changing yourself, the less time you have trying to change others. When you change, your circumstances and the people around you will change.

When I made the decision to change my circle, I considered those who were uplifting and those who came across as negative and confrontational. This includes family members who bring negative energy. This is where you have to be not only honest, but shrewd in your decision. This is harsh, I know. But burning bridges is okay—it ensures you move forward and don't go back. You know who you can trust, and those are the people you should invest your time with.

How does picking your circle work? Start off with the people who have been there for you in the past. Have they given you sound advice which moves you in a positive direction? Do they add value to your life? Have they helped build your confidence? Write these questions down, then list the names of people you trust to be in your circle. Think of who you want to become. Now imagine dropping 200 people from your social media who don't align with that vision.

Think of that version of yourself which you can admire; the strong, healthy, and successful person you have imagined in the past. It isn't difficult. You have seen this person before. Then think about the events you truly enjoy attending. Perhaps a place where you can be you. You don't have to pretend; this is the place where you can express your thoughts without judgment or fear. Seek out communities, events, or groups where people are already living the life you aspire to. Growth happens when you show up where growth-minded people gather. Remember one key element: your privacy falls on your shoulders. Being the best version of yourself includes the people you spend time with.

This is something I wish I would have learned at an early age. You have the power to create the life you want—but it starts with choosing the right people to walk alongside you. Since starting this journey of transformation, doors have opened that I never imagined. A change in attitude changes everything. I've written and published two books, launched my own podcast, and connected with people earning six and seven figures—opportunities that came because I changed my circle. Successful people don't invest their time with negative people. Put a smile on your face and show up as someone worth knowing.

Depression doesn't have to be a life sentence. This is where I was when my mentor found me. The journey hasn't been easy, but the joy of becoming a new creation makes every struggle worth it. Failure is not an option. What do you truly want? If you can prove that a negative attitude leads to a successful life, I'd love to see the research.

## Reflection Questions:

1. Who are the five people you spend the most time with? Are they lifting you or pulling you down?

_____

_____

2. What qualities do you want to develop in yourself? Who in your life already embodies those qualities?

_____

_____

3. Think about your current environment (work, social circles, home). Is it supporting the future you want to create?

_____

_____

4. What is one relationship or environment you need to change to move toward the life you desire?

_____

_____

## Chapter 9

# The Source

We are all connected to Spirit. If this were not true, we would not exist. Yet one of our greatest failures is believing we are separate from God. This false belief keeps us from discovering our true purpose and pursuing the dreams placed in our hearts. The moment we accept the lie of separation, we begin living close to our potential.

As it is written in the Bible, Jesus says that he is the vine, and we are the branches. Many people believe we are separate from God, but Jesus himself said, "Of my own, I can do nothing; it is the Father in me who does the work." If Jesus—who walked this earth as a man—acknowledged his connection to the Father, how much more do we need to recognize our own connection to our Source? He demonstrated the truth of connection through his words and actions. We must follow that same understanding.

You have a specific purpose with unique talents to succeed in that purpose. But here is what most people miss: your purpose is revealed through your desires. The dreams you carry are not random—they are invitations from God, showing you the path to fulfillment. God has promised to give us the desires of our hearts. Those desires were not placed there by accident.

During my time in the Navy, I believed my purpose as a leader was to develop the sailors under my charge for success, whether they stayed in the Navy or transitioned to the civilian sector. I had clarity. I had direction. But after I separated from the Navy, I felt lost and uncertain when it came to seeking employment. I did not know what my purpose was anymore. Prayer was not a daily practice during this period of time.

Looking back, I can see the connection clearly: when I stopped connecting with God, I lost my sense of purpose. This is what happens when we live as though we are separate. We drift. We feel lost. We settle for less than what we were created for. But when we reconnect—when we pray, listen, and trust—everything changes.

Your thoughts, dreams, and ideas do not come from nowhere. They come from your connection to the Source. God speaks to you through the desires He places in your heart. When you quiet your mind and listen, you will hear His guidance. This connection is not reserved for a chosen few—it is available to everyone who seeks it.

How do you explain the creation of the universe? The Bible tells us God spoke the Earth into existence. There is an energy that flows through all things, sustaining the planets, the stars, the very breath in your lungs. Science has yet to explain where this energy comes from, but we know the Source. We are not separate from it—we are part of it.

Consider this: God created man in His own image. God is not a physical form but Spirit. So when the Bible says we are made in His image, it means we are spiritual beings with intellect and creative power. You have been gifted with a mind that learns, a body that acts, and a Spirit that connects you to the divine. We are all created equal. Why would God create Himself to be less than or greater than Himself?

He would not. We each have the same access to the Source. Yet so many people live as though they do not. Some boast about being more intelligent than others. Some believe themselves to be less.

But the truth is, no one has been denied opportunities to learn, to succeed, or to be happy. We have been given free will—not to do whatever we want, but to think whatever we want. And what we think determines what we create. Those who have more in life learned how to ask for more. They imagine a more abundant life and believe it is possible.

As a parent or a partner, do you not wish to provide encouragement for the success of those you love? God desires the same for you. The promise for prosperity, hope, and a future is the plan written for you in the Bible. The dream you have in your heart is there for a reason. What is your dream?

How do you feel when you imagine it being completed? Years ago, I dreamed of visiting Australia. Hearing stories from people who had been there left me wishing for that experience. In 1997, when I went on my last deployment overseas, that dream came true. We visited Perth, Australia, and Hobart, Tasmania.

Dreams do come true when you believe in them and take action. But here is the deeper truth: pursuing that dream was not just about travel. It was about learning to trust the desires God placed in my heart. It was about believing that what seemed impossible could become possible. Your dreams work the same way.

They are not just wishes—they are assignments. They reveal who you are meant to become. Your identity is not defined by your failures, mistakes, or bad choices. These are simply experiences that bring you back to God, reminding you of your connection to the Source. Your identity is predetermined.

Your experiences are lessons that help you learn who you were created to be. Pursuing your goals and dreams will help you discover your true self. Your journey is unique to you, and staying connected on a spiritual level will take you in the direction that affords the greatest impact for the people you meet. When you remain connected, the right opportunities will present themselves at the right time. This is not a coincidence—it is divine guidance.

So many people place their dreams on the shelf because they believe they are impossible. But with God, nothing is impossible. The question is not whether you can accomplish your dreams. The question is: do you believe you are connected to the Source that makes all things possible? Your belief determines your reality.

Stop living like you are separate. You are not alone. You are not powerless. You are a branch connected to the vine, and the same power that created the universe flows through you. Connect with God through prayer.

Listen for His guidance. Trust the desires He has placed in your heart. Believe that what seems impossible is only impossible when you try to do it alone. When you acknowledge your connection to the Source, limitations disappear. Faith becomes the foundation of everything you do.

When you reconnect to your Source, everything changes. Clarity returns. Purpose is revealed. Dreams become reality. This is not theory—this is truth. And it is waiting for you the moment you stop believing in the lie of separation and start living in the reality of connection.

Your dreams are not accidents. They are invitations. Will you answer?

## Reflection Questions:

1. What dream has God placed in your heart that you have been ignoring?

_____

_____

2. Do you believe nothing is impossible with God?

_____

_____

3. What would become possible if you truly believed?

_____

_____

4. What is one step you can take today to pursue the dream you have been putting off?

_____

_____

# Conclusion

When we began this journey together, we explored the hidden power within you—the power of your mind to shape your reality, to overcome conditioning, and to break free from the limitations you have accepted as truth. Like the elephant tied to a rope, you have been stronger than you realized all along. The rope was never the problem. Your belief in the rope was.

We have walked through the principles that separate those who succeed from those who remain stuck. You have learned that gratitude and forgiveness are not just nice ideas—they are the foundation for freedom and growth. You have discovered how to create your world by writing down your goals with deadlines, giving your mind a clear target to pursue. You have explored what it means to love unconditionally, starting with the person in the mirror, and releasing the expectations that create friction in your relationships.

Each chapter has offered you tools, but tools are only valuable when you use them. The hidden power, the grateful heart, the written goal, the unconditional love—these are not concepts to admire from a distance. They are practices to implement daily.

The question is not whether you understand them. The question is: will you live them?

I will not pretend I have always known these truths. For years, I was the person playing video games for hours, neglecting what truly mattered, wondering why success eluded me. I was the guy who needed a few drinks just to ask a woman to dance because the fear of rejection controlled me. I carried anger from my past disappointments for years, letting bitterness and unforgiveness anchor me to the past. I built walls because of criticism from family, became cynical and rigid, and refused guidance when it was offered as I leaned on my own understanding.

The turning point came when I attended Tony Robbins seminars in 2020 and began studying personal development seriously. That is when I learned about gratitude, forgiveness, and the power of the mind. Most importantly, this is where I discovered my past experiences were the problems holding me back. Not believing in myself because of the criticism I received from people I knew. When I asked myself the question that changed everything: "What kind of business could I build if I spent as much time and energy on it as I do this video game?"

That question led me to coaching. It led me to pursuing my purpose—helping others succeed. It led me to the friend who introduced me to the publisher of this book. None of these opportunities would have existed if I had remained the bitter, angry, fearful version of myself.

Today, I can approach people with confidence. I can receive feedback without defensiveness. I have learned to love unconditionally and let people go when it is time. I have forgiven the past and planted seeds of love without demanding a harvest. I am not perfect—I am still learning to be coachable, still growing, still discovering—but I am free. And if these principles transformed me, they could transform you too.

Prosperity is not about money or material things. This is a common misconception which we have been conditioned to believe. The relationships you cultivate is your prosperity. The way people feel in your presence, the connections which leave you feeling loved and appreciated.

True prosperity is waking up with peace instead of anxiety. It is living with a purpose that excites you, not a job that drains you. It is being comfortable in your own skin, no longer seeking validation from others to feel worthy. Prosperity is the freedom to forgive quickly, to love without conditions, and to pursue your dreams without fear holding you back.

I have had moments where I possessed material things but felt empty. And I have had moments with nothing in my bank account but everything in my heart—sitting with a friend, coaching someone through a breakthrough, or simply recognizing that I am learning more about who I am and not the person living a lie. Those moments are prosperity. They cannot be bought, stolen, or lost. They are earned through inner work, through choosing growth over comfort, through becoming the person you were created to be.

When you recognize money does not solve your problems nor does it strengthen your relationships, you will see life differently. Remember this one simple thing: you came into the world empty handed and you will leave the same way. Seek your purpose, invest in yourself, learn new skills which are marketable, and take up a hobby which allows you to disconnect from the stress of the day.

So where do you go from here? This book is not meant to sit on a shelf as inspiration you once felt. It is a manual for transformation, but only if you use it.

Start with the reflection questions at the end of each chapter. Do not just read them—answer them. Write them down. Sit with them. These questions are designed to unlock the hidden power within you, but only if you engage with them honestly.

Pick one chapter that resonated most deeply with you and commit to practicing that principle for the next 30 days. If it is gratitude, start every morning by naming three things you are grateful for. If it is goal-setting, write down your goal with a deadline today. If it is forgiveness, identify one person you need to release and let them go. One chapter. One practice. Thirty days. That is how transformation begins.

Find a mentor or an accountability partner—someone who is further along the path you want to walk, or someone walking alongside you who will hold you accountable. Growth happens in community, not isolation. You were not meant to do this alone.

Finally, remember that growth is not a destination—it is a journey. There will be setbacks. There will be days when you fall back into old patterns. That is not failure. That is being human. The question is whether you will keep going. Whether you will test your strength against the rope one more time.

The elephant stops pulling because it believes the rope is

stronger. But you? You now know the truth. The rope was never real. The limitations were beliefs, not facts. And beliefs can be changed.

The journey ahead will not be easy. There will be people who criticize you, who say you are chasing impossible dreams, who remind you of your failures. Let them. Their doubts are not your truth. Their limitations are not your reality. You are not bound by their beliefs about what is possible.

You already possess everything you need. The hidden power has always been there, waiting for you to recognize it. The mind that imagines failure can also imagine success. The heart that has felt pain also feels joy. The same strength that taught you to walk without instruction, that heals your body without conscious effort, is the strength that will carry you toward your dreams.

I believe in you—not because I know you personally, but because I know the principles in this book work. I have lived them. I have seen them transform my life and the lives of countless others. If you commit to these practices, if you choose growth over comfort, if you test your strength instead of accepting the rope—your life will change. Not someday. Not when conditions are perfect. Now.

So here is my final question for you: Will you continue to believe in the rope, or will you finally test your strength? Will you keep listening to the critics, or will you prove to yourself, not to them that you are capable of more than you ever imagined? The hidden power is yours. Trust in God, He is your source of strength.

## About the Author

"**Michael Chavez** spent decades behind walls he didn't realize he'd built, walls constructed from a single, devastating label: *not good enough*. Those three words shaped every decision, every relationship, every limitation he accepted as truth. He kept people at arm's length, hid his true self, yet desperately sought validation from those who saw little value in his life.

After 25 years of Biblical study and personal development, Michael discovered his depression came not from circumstances, but from accepting a false identity built on other people's labels.

TRANSFORMING DEPRESSION INTO A PROSPEROUS LIFE

The transformation was radical. At 60, Michael became a published author, international keynote speaker, and left his career to build a business helping others break free from the same prison. As a retired Navy Chief Petty Officer and Founder of KinSpired Goal Setters, he helps people reclaim their true identity and step into prosperity."

To contact Michael Chavez for Speaking Engagements, Email address:

Michael.chavez8569@gmail.com

Website: https://michael-chavez-pgi-consultant.mailchimpsites.com/

LinkedIn www.linkedin.com/in/michael-chavez-ceoksgs

Facebook @KinSpiredGoalSetters

Instagram @michael_chavez99

Made in the USA
Coppell, TX
20 January 2026

66182680R00056